T0348419

Tim Chester

The Lord's Prayer

Talking to Our Father

GOOD BOOK GUIDE

7-Session Bible Study

/

The Lord's Prayer: Talking to Our Father
A Good Book Guide
© Tim Chester, 2020.
This edition printed 2025.

Published by The Good Book Company

thegoodbook.com | thegoodbook.co.uk
thegoodbook.com.au | thegoodbook.co.nz | thegoodbook.co.in

A CIP catalogue record for this book is available from the British Library.

Design by André Parker and Drew McCall

ISBN: 9781802541939 | JOB-008042 | Printed in India

Contents

 # Introduction

One of the Bible writers described God's word as "a lamp for my feet, a light on my path" (Psalm 119:105, NIV). God gave us the Bible to tell us about who he is and what he wants for us. He speaks through it by his Spirit and lights our way through life.

That means that we need to look carefully at the Bible and uncover its meaning—but we also need to apply what we've discovered to our lives.

Good Book Guides are designed to help you do just that. The sessions in this book are interactive and easy to lead. They're perfect for use in groups or for personal study.

Let's take a look at what is included in each session.

Talkabout: Every session starts with an ice-breaker question, designed to get people talking around a subject that links to the Bible study.

Investigate: These questions help you explore what the passage is about.

Apply: These questions are designed to get you thinking practically: what does this Bible teaching mean for you and your church?

Explore More: These optional sections help you to go deeper or to explore another part of the Bible which connects with the main passage.

Getting Personal: These sections are a chance for personal reflection. Some groups may feel comfortable discussing these, but you may prefer to look at them quietly as individuals instead—or leave them out.

Pray: Here, you're invited to pray in the light of the truths and challenges you've seen in the study.

Each session is also designed to be easily split into two! Watch out for the **Apply** section that comes halfway through, and stop there if you haven't got time to do the whole thing in one go.

In the back of the book, you'll find a **Leader's Guide**, which provides helpful notes on every question, along with everything else that group leaders need in order to facilitate a great session and help the group uncover the riches of God's light-giving word.

Why Study the Lord's Prayer?

"Lord, teach us to pray."

That's the question the disciples once asked Jesus (Luke 11:1). Perhaps it's a question you ask. *How should I pray? What should I say? How can I pray better?*

Jesus' answer to the question posed by his disciples was the prayer we call "the Lord's Prayer". In Luke's Gospel Jesus introduces it with the words, "When you pray, say…" It suggests a form of words we can repeat. Perhaps you say it in your church each Sunday. In Matthew's Gospel Jesus introduces it with the words, "This, then, is how you should pray". This suggests a pattern or framework we can use to shape our own prayers. One great way of praying is to go through the Lord's Prayer line by line, expanding on each phrase in turn with your own specific words of praise, confession or request. It's something you can do on your own or with a group.

This study guide is designed to help you to do this. We'll study the Lord's Prayer—along with other passages from Matthew's Gospel that shed light on it—so that we can repeat it more intelligently and so we can allow it to shape our own prayers.

But prayer is also a great window onto who God is and what he's done for us. This works in both directions. A better understanding of God helps us to pray. But prayer can also be like the training ground where we discover more about God and his purposes. Prayer embeds the knowledge of God deep into our souls.

The Lord's Prayer is a *short* prayer. It takes less than 30 seconds to say and that's without rushing. We've all got time to do that each day! But the Lord's Prayer is not a *small* prayer. If you say it with meaning, then this prayer will enlarge your vision, expand your horizons and transform your life.

The Lord's Prayer

MATTHEW 6:9-13

Our Father in heaven,
hallowed be your name,
your kingdom come,
your will be done,
on earth as it is in heaven.
Give us today our daily bread.
And forgive us our debts,
as we also have forgiven our debtors.
And lead us not into temptation,
but deliver us from the evil one.

COMMON WORSHIP*

Our Father in heaven,
hallowed be your name,
your kingdom come,
your will be done,
on earth as in heaven.
Give us today our daily bread.
Forgive us our sins
as we forgive those who sin against us.
Lead us not into temptation
but deliver us from evil.
For the kingdom, the power, and the glory are yours
now and for ever.
Amen.

* This is the version used in many churches. From Common Worship: Services and Prayers for the Church of England (Church House, 2000), page 36.

Our Father in Heaven

Matthew 6:5-9 and 7:7-11

Talkabout

1. What words do you associate with the word "prayer"?

• What attitudes are revealed by those words?

Investigate

📖 **Read Matthew 6:5-8**

DICTIONARY

Hypocrite (v 5): someone who says one thing and does another.
Synagogue (v 5): a Jewish temple.

Pagans (v 7): a believer in Greek and Roman gods.

---

2. Twice in these verses Jesus says, "When you pray, do not…" What wrong ways to pray does Jesus identify?

3. Why do the people Jesus describes pray this way?

4. How does the way that Jesus describes God serve to correct those wrong ways of praying?

Apply

5. When you pray as a group, how might you be tempted to pray…
   • like the hypocrites Jesus describes in verse 5?

   • like the babbling pagans of verse 7?

6. How can you avoid doing so?

God the Father delights to hear us pray. Do you delight in praying? What do your prayers suggest about the way you view God? Does the way you pray in private reflect the way you pray in public?

Investigate

7. If God already knows what we need (as 6:8 says), why do you think Jesus encourages us to pray?

📖 **Read Matthew 7:7-11**

8. What is the promise in verses 7-8?

9. What is Jesus' argument in verses 9-11?

Many of us have prayed prayers which God has not answered in the way we wanted. Often these prayers are prayed in times of turmoil and grief.

We need to remember that God is a loving and wise Father who is committed to our ultimate good and that he has displayed this commitment in the gift of his Son on the cross.

So, although God does not always give us what we want, he does always give us what is good. We must not let these qualifications blunt this big invitation to bring our requests and questions to God.

10. How does this relationship with God as Father differ from the expectations of the hypocrites and babblers in Matthew 6:5-8?

Explore More | OPTIONAL

📖 Read Galatians 4:4-7

- How does God the Son change our relationship with God?
- How does God the Spirit change our relationship with God?
- How does this affect our praying?

Apply

📖 Read Matthew 6:9

11. How will our prayers be shaped by knowing that God reigns from heaven?

12. How will our prayers be shaped by knowing that God is our Father?

Getting Personal | OPTIONAL

Pause to pray now. Start by hearing the words of Matthew 7:7 as an invitation to you from your heavenly Father: "Ask and it will be given to you; seek and you will find; knock and the door will be opened to you."

Pray

Praise God that he reigns from heaven and so he can answer our prayers.

Praise God that he is our Father and so he will answer our prayers.

Share the needs for which you would like prayer and then let these truths shape your requests.

2

Hallowed Be Your Name

Matthew 1:18 – 2:12 and 28:16-20

Talkabout

1. Do you think your name suits you? Why, or why not?

Investigate

📖 **Read Matthew 1:18-25**

2. What names will be given to the promised baby?

3. What do these names tell us about the baby?

📖 **Read Matthew 2:1-12**

4. Why have the Magi come to find Jesus? What do they do when they find him?

5. Why does Herod say he wants to find Jesus?

- What light does verse 12 shed on that?

📖 **Read Matthew 6:9**

"Hallowed be your name" is a prayer that God's name might be regarded as holy or worshipped. The names of Jesus reveal who Jesus is and why he is worth worshipping.

Yet the Jewish king, the chief priests and the teachers of the law do not worship Jesus at his birth. Instead it falls to strangers—non-Jews who are not part of God's people—to bring him the worship he deserves.

Apply

6. If we started with worship more often, how do you think the rest of our prayers would change?

Getting Personal | OPTIONAL

Are your prayers centred on your needs or God's glory? Do the priorities of your life mirror the priorities of your prayers?

Investigate

Having looked at the first chapters of Matthew's Gospel, next we fast-forward to the very end.

📖 **Read Matthew 28:16-20**

7. What do the disciples do when they see the risen Jesus?

8. What reasons are there to worship Jesus in these verses?

9. What will those who worship him do?

10. What does that have to do with God's name?

Explore More | OPTIONAL

📖 Read Matthew 15:1-9

Verses 8-9 describe people whose *lips* "hallow" God's name, but whose *lives* do not.

- Where did the Pharisees go wrong?
- How might we fall into the trap of honouring God's name with our lips but not with our lives?

The version of the Lord's Prayer used in most churches ends with the words, "For the kingdom, the power, and the glory are yours now and for ever". This line is not part of the original prayer recorded in Matthew 6 or Luke 11. But these words are consistent with the climax of Matthew's Gospel where Jesus is given all authority, and, because he has received all authority, he sends us to call the nations to submit to his kingship and worship his glory.

Matthew's Gospel begins with the nations (in the form of the Magi) worshipping Jesus and ends with the disciples being sent to call the nations to worship Jesus. This is related to the prayer "Hallowed be your name": we are not only expressing our own worship but also praying that others might do the same.

Getting Personal | OPTIONAL

How can you pray for God's name to be hallowed in your life:

- in what you say?
- in what you do?

Apply

11. Think about your church: what would it mean to pray for God's name to be hallowed there?

12. Think about your neighbourhood and your country: how can you pray for God's name to be hallowed there?

Pray

Pick some of the Bible's names for Jesus and turn them into prayers of praise.

Here are some options to start you off: Jesus is Saviour, Immanuel, the Messiah, the Good Shepherd, the Altogether Lovely, the Word of God, our Great High Priest, the Son of God, the Lamb of God, the Bread of Life, and the Hope of the Nations.

3

Your Kingdom Come

Matthew 13:1-23 and 13:31-32

Talkabout

1. "On Sunday morning I sing about Jesus being King, but on Monday morning I only get grief from my colleagues if I speak about Jesus to them." Do you ever experience a gap like this between Sunday and Monday morning? Why is this?

When God first created the world, humanity lived under God's kingdom or rule. It was a kingdom of peace, plenty and protection. But humanity has rejected God's kingdom. We think we will be freer without God. Instead we have become enslaved to sin and subject to God's judgment. But God has promised to restore his kingdom through his King: Jesus.

The problem is that the final restoration of God's kingdom will mean judgment for those who have rebelled against him—and that includes us all. So before that final restoration, Jesus first came to bring forgiveness and peace with God.

Investigate

📖 **Read Matthew 13:1-9, 18-23**

2. How does the kingdom of heaven grow within history?

3. In what negative ways do people respond to the message of Jesus?

4. In what positive ways do people respond to the message of Jesus?

5. How does Jesus apply this parable? What command does he give (v 9)?

6. How would you summarise "the message about the kingdom" (v 19) in your own words?

Explore More | OPTIONAL

📖 **Read Matthew 27:41-42**

- How did the religious leaders challenge Jesus to prove he is God's promised King?
- What did Jesus do instead?

The coming of the kingdom of God means judgment for rebels. But in stage one of the kingdom's coming, judgment does not fall on rebels. Instead judgment falls on the King himself, in our place at the cross.

Apply

7. Jesus applies this parable by commanding us to hear (v 9). Who do you know who has not yet heard about Jesus? How could you make sure they get the chance to hear and respond?

Investigate

📖 **Read Matthew 13:31-32**

8. What does this image tell us about the kingdom of heaven in the present?

9. What does it tell us about the kingdom of heaven in the future?

10. In what ways do you think this future has already begun to happen?

Jesus is promising that although the kingdom looks small and insignificant now, one day it will come fully. When Jesus returns, those who reject God will be judged, and God's rule of peace and plenty will be restored.

Explore More | OPTIONAL

📖 **Read 2 Peter 3:3-9**

- How does Peter counter the accusation that the kingdom of God is never going to come in judgment? What reason does he give for the delay?

📖 **Read 2 Peter 3:10-13**

- What will the fulfilment of God's kingdom look like?

Apply

📖 **Read Matthew 6:10**

When we pray "Your kingdom come", we are praying for two things at once: first, the gradual spread of God's kingdom in the present as people hear Jesus' words, repent and come under God's rule; and second, the ultimate return of Jesus in glory.

11. What specific things could you pray about when you ask for God's kingdom to come:
    - in the present?

    - in the future?

Getting Personal | OPTIONAL

📖 **Read Matthew 6:19-20**

Think about what you are storing up for yourself. What do your priorities in life reveal about your attitude towards the kingdom of heaven?

12. How should the coming of the kingdom in the future shape our attitude to the kingdom in the present?

Pray

Pray for opportunities to share the message of the kingdom with unbelieving friends.

Pray for the evangelistic initiatives in your church.

Pray for the missionaries supported by your church.

4

Your Will Be Done

Matthew 26:36-46

Talkabout

1. How do children react when they don't get their own way? How do adults react?

Investigate

📖 **Read Matthew 26:36-46**

2. How does Matthew describe the emotions of Jesus in these verses?

3. Why is Jesus feeling these emotions?

4. What does Jesus request in his prayer of verse 39?

- What difference do you think it made to add "Yet not as I will, but as you will"?

5. What is the difference between the prayers in verse 39 and verse 42?

Apply

"Your will be done" in verse 42 is word-for-word the same as "Your will be done" in the Lord's Prayer.

6. How does the story of Gethsemane help us to see what it means for us to pray this?

The Lord's Prayer is an act of submission to God's will—both obeying him (submitting to his moral will, the way he wants us to live) and accepting our circumstances (submitting to his sovereign will, his control over all things).

It is okay to ask God to change the circumstances of our lives (as Jesus does in verse 39). But if God does not change our circumstances then we must submit to his will.

7. When things don't go our way, how might we behave if we are not submitting to God's sovereign will?

Getting Personal | OPTIONAL

Are you bitter because you struggle to accept the sovereign will of God?

Are you over-busy because you're trying to be in control instead of entrusting your concerns to God's control?

Do you feel justified in not doing what God wants, because he's not doing what you want?

Remind yourself who God is. Remind yourself of Jesus in Gethsemane. Ask God to help you say, "Yet not as I will, but as you will".

Investigate

📖 Read Matthew 6:9-13

The Lord's Prayer contains three requests for our needs (v 11-13). But it begins with three requests for God's glory (v 9-10).

8. What attitude do you need in order to start a prayer with these requests?

9. How does the phrase "as it is in heaven" alter the way you think about these requests?

10. How is praying "your will be done" similar to praying "hallowed be your name" and "your kingdom come"? How is it different?

Getting Personal | OPTIONAL

Think about your prayers. Do they reflect the balance of the Lord's Prayer? Do you begin with God or with yourself?

Explore More | OPTIONAL

Submitting to God's will can be hard, especially when it involves suffering.

📖 **Read 1 Peter 2:21-25**

- How does the submission of Jesus help us?

Apply

11. In what areas of life do you find it hard to put God first? Why?

12. How could we remind ourselves to put God first?

Pray

Use the following passages to help you pray for one another.

"Now may the God of peace, who through the blood of the eternal covenant brought back from the dead our Lord Jesus, that great Shepherd of the sheep, equip you with everything good for doing his will, and may he work in us what is pleasing to him, through Jesus Christ, to whom be glory for ever and ever. Amen." (Hebrews 13:20-21)

May the God of all grace, who called you to his eternal glory in Christ, after you have suffered a little while, restore you and make you strong, firm and steadfast. To him be the power for ever and ever. Amen.

(Adapted from 1 Peter 5:10-11)

5

Give Us Today Our Daily Bread

Matthew 6:25-34

Talkabout

1. What do you worry about?

Investigate

📖 **Read Matthew 6:25-30**

DICTIONARY

Reap (v 26): harvest crops.

Spin (v 28): make loose wool into yarn.

---

2. Jesus repeatedly tells us not to worry in these verses. What reason does he give for not worrying:
   - in verse 25?

- in verse 27?

3. Look at verse 30. What is the root cause of worry?

4. What does Jesus tell us to do in verses 26 and 28? How does this help counter worry?

5. Have you had experiences of looking at the world around you and being filled with wonder or reassured of God's care?

6. How does Jesus describe God in these verses?

- Reflect on each word of this phrase. How does it help us even more?

Explore More | OPTIONAL

Matthew 14 tells us about a time when the disciples were full of worry and fear.

📖 **Read Matthew 14:13-21**

- What lesson should the disciples have learned from this story?

📖 **Read Matthew 14:22-26**

- How did they react the next time they were in trouble?

📖 **Read Matthew 14:27-33**

- How did Peter show faith? What caused him to stop having faith?

Apply

📖 **Read Matthew 6:11**

7. In what ways does the prayer "give us today our daily bread" express the attitude that Jesus is telling us to have in Matthew 6:25?

Praying for "daily" bread made sense in Jesus' day because life felt precarious and food could not easily be stored. But it is just as important for us to pray for our daily needs because we need to be reminded that we are dependent on God. We may get our food from a supermarket and store it in a fridge, but this prayer reminds us that God is the ultimate provider.

Getting Personal | OPTIONAL

Think about the last time you got anxious. How might your perspective have been changed by…

- thinking of God as "your heavenly Father"?
- praying "Give us today our daily bread"?

Investigate

📖 **Read Matthew 6:31-34**

8. According to Jesus, what is to be our priority?

9. What distracts us from this priority?

10. What do we need to remind ourselves of in order not to be distracted?

Apply

11. What might it look like in practice for us to make the kingdom of God our priority?

12. When we pray "Give us today our daily bread", what are we asking for?

• How does that help us to have the right priorities?

Getting Personal | OPTIONAL

What steps could you take this week to make God's kingdom your priority?

Pray

"Cast all your anxiety on [God] because he cares for you." (1 Peter 5:7)

Make a list of the things that cause you anxiety. Then hand them over one by one in prayer to God because he cares for you.

Or invite everyone in the group to share one thing that makes them anxious. Then pray both for God's provision for your needs and God's peace for your hearts.

6

Forgive Us Our Sins

Matthew 9:1-8 and 18:21-35

Talkabout

1. When was the last time someone forgave you? What did it feel like?

Investigate

📖 **Read Matthew 9:1-8**

DICTIONARY

Blaspheming (v 3): speaking
disrespectfully or falsely about God.

---

2. What is the immediate need of the man who is brought to Jesus? What
is the ultimate need of the man?

3. What does his response to the man make us think of Jesus?

4. How does Jesus respond to the religious leaders?

5. Do you think the crowd are right in the way they respond to Jesus?

Apply

6. If you're a Christian, then all your sins—past, present and future—are forgiven through the cross. So why does Jesus encourage us to continue to pray "forgive us our sins"?

Getting Personal | OPTIONAL

"Search me, God, and know my heart;
   test me and know my anxious thoughts.
 See if there is any offensive way in me,
   and lead me in the way everlasting." (Psalm 139:23-24)

Take time to review your life. Ask God to reveal your "hidden faults" (Psalm 19:12). Do you need to repent of sinful behaviours, attitudes or habits? Come to Jesus for mercy. Ask him to forgive you. And hear him say, "Take heart ... your sins are forgiven" (Matthew 9:2).

The Lord's Prayer links *receiving* forgiveness with *showing* forgiveness: "And forgive us our debts, as we also have forgiven our debtors" (Matthew 6.12).

Does this mean that showing forgiveness is the reason for our forgiveness by God—we earn forgiveness by being forgiving? Or is showing forgiveness the evidence of our forgiveness by God? Which comes first—our mercy or God's mercy?

Jesus provides his own commentary on this in the following passage.

Investigate

📖 **Read Matthew 18:21-35**

7. Think about what the different elements of the story represent. What is Jesus telling us about…
   • what sin is like?

   • what is happening when God has mercy?

8. How should the king's forgiveness make the servant feel about himself?

   • Does it actually have that effect (v 28-30)?

9. How do the other people in the story react to the servant's refusal to forgive?

10. According to the story, which comes first—our mercy or God's mercy? What is the evidence that we have received forgiveness from God?

We do not earn God's forgiveness by being forgiving—God's forgiveness comes first. But showing forgiveness is a good sign that we have truly accepted God's forgiveness and repented of sin.

This is why Jesus says, "For if you forgive other people when they sin against you, your heavenly Father will also forgive you. But if you do not forgive others their sins, your Father will not forgive your sins" (Matthew 6:14-15).

If we don't forgive others, we are thinking of ourselves as more righteous than them, when in fact we are just as sinful. We are effectively turning our back on God and his mercy—just like the servant in Jesus' parable.

📖 **Read Matthew 6:12**

Explore More | OPTIONAL

The word "debt" is, as we have seen, a powerful picture for sin. Sin is failing to meet our obligations towards God and we lack the resources to repay what we owe. But the word "debt" also alludes to the jubilee laws of Deuteronomy 15.

📖 **Read Deuteronomy 15:1-15**

- What does God tell his people to do in verses 1, 10, 11 and 12?
- What reason does God give for these commands in verse 15?
- How does this help us to understand what it means to pray this line of the Lord's Prayer?

Apply

11. How can we reflect God's mercy in the way we treat other people?

12. What kind of person are we asking God to make us into when we pray, "Forgive us our sins as we forgive those who sin against us"?

Getting Personal | OPTIONAL

If someone were to review your reactions when other people wrong you or assess your generosity to those in need, what would they conclude?

Would they notice a distinctive attitude in you? Would they conclude that you have received mercy from God?

Is there anyone with whom you need to be reconciled?

Pray

"Almighty and most merciful Father,
we have wandered and strayed from your ways
like lost sheep.
We have followed too much the devices and desires
of our own hearts.
We have offended against your holy laws.
We have left undone those things
that we ought to have done;
and we have done those things
that we ought not to have done;
and there is no health in us.
But you, O Lord, have mercy upon us sinners.

Spare those who confess their faults.
Restore those who are penitent,
according to your promises declared to mankind
in Christ Jesus our Lord.
And grant, O most merciful Father, for his sake,
that we may live a disciplined, righteous and godly life,
to the glory of your holy name.
Amen."

> *From the Book of Common Prayer. This version is from Common Worship: Services and Prayers for the Church of England (Church House, 2000), page 129.*

7

Lead Us Not Into Temptation

Matthew 4:1-11 and 26:40-41

Talkabout

1. What has been your worst exam experience? What does it feel like to fail a test?

The word "temptation" literally means "testing" and describes a broad range of trials, not just being enticed to sin (though it can include being enticed to sin, as Matthew 4:1 indicates).

Elsewhere the Bible tells us to rejoice when we face trials (James 1:2-3). So we are praying here to be delivered not in the sense of being spared trials, but in the sense of spared from sinning or giving up when we are tested (delivered "out from" or "through" temptation).

Investigate

📖 **Read Matthew 4:1-11 and 6:13**

2. What similarities are there between these verses?

3. What temptations does Jesus face?

4. How does Jesus overcome these temptations?

Explore More | OPTIONAL

📖 **Read 1 Corinthians 10:13**

- What does this verse say about temptation?
- How does it help us understand what it means to pray, "Lead us not into temptation, but deliver us from the evil one"?

📖 **Read Matthew 26:33-35, 69-75**

In Matthew 4 Jesus was tested three times and remained faithful. Here Peter is tested three times and fails each time.

📖 **Read Matthew 26:40-41**

5. What would have helped Peter not to fail when tested and fall when tempted?

6. Why do you think he didn't do as he was told (but slept instead, v 43)?

Apply

7. What key ways of resisting temptation have we seen?

- Are these the things we usually do when we face testing times, or do we try other things instead?

Getting Personal | OPTIONAL

In what specific ways are you being tempted or tested at the moment?

What Bible passages or gospel truths could you use to help you remain faithful?

How does the faithfulness of Jesus comfort you in these situations?

Investigate

8. Look again at Matthew 4:1 and 6:13. How does what happened to Jesus differ from what we are told to pray for ourselves?

9. Why do you think that is? What is special about Jesus?

10. Jesus' testing echoes the story of the fall in Genesis 3 and the story of the Israelites' time in the wilderness in Exodus (for example, Exodus 17:1-7).
   • What are the similarities?

   • What is the big difference?

Jesus replays the story of humanity and the story of Israel. Uniquely, he passes Satan's test—and he does so on behalf of all his people. Through the faithfulness of Jesus, every Christian has passed the "entrance exam" required to enter God's kingdom.

Here are some other passages in which Matthew uses the word "evil" or "wicked": Matthew 9:2-4; 12:35, 12:39; 13:19; 13:38; 15:19; 18:32.

11. How do these passages illuminate what it means to pray to be delivered from evil?

Apply

12. When we do fail and fall, how should we feel and respond?

Getting Personal | OPTIONAL

Think back across all our studies on the Lord's Prayer. Using it as a framework for our prayers will change the way we pray and the way we live, in lots of different ways.

Which part of the Lord's Prayer is the biggest challenge for you when it comes to the way you pray?

Pray

Say the first line of the Lord's Prayer and then have two or three people expand on it with their own specific prayers of praise, confession or request. Then move on to the next line and repeat the process until you have "prayed through" the whole of the Lord's Prayer together.

The Lord's Prayer

Prayer

Talking to Our Father

LEADER'S
GUIDE

Leader's Guide: Introduction

This Leader's Guide includes guidance for every question. It will provide background information and help you if you get stuck. For each session, you'll also find the following:

The Big Idea: The main point of the session, in brief. This is what you should be aiming to have fixed in people's minds by the end of the session!

Summary: An overview of the passage you're reading together.

Optional Extra: Usually this is an introductory activity that ties in with the main theme of the Bible study and is designed to break the ice at the beginning of a session. Or it may be a "homework project" that people can tackle during the week.

Occasionally the Leader's Guide includes an extra follow-up question, printed in *italics*. This doesn't appear in the main study guide but could be a useful add-on to help your group get to the answer or go deeper.

Here are a few key principles to bear in mind as you prepare to lead:

- Don't just read out the answers from the Leader's Guide. Ideally, you want the group to discover these answers from the Bible for themselves.

- Keep drawing people back to the passage you're studying. People may come up with answers based on their experiences or on teaching they've heard in the past, but the point of this study is to listen to God's word itself—so keep directing your group to look at the text.

- Make sure everyone finishes the session knowing how the passage is relevant for them. We do Bible study so that our lives can be changed by what we hear from God's word. So, **Apply** questions aren't just an add-on—they're a vital part of the session.

Finally, remember that your group is unique! You should feel free to use this Good Book Guide in a way that works for them. If they're a quiet bunch, you might want to spend longer on the **Talkabout** question. If they love to get creative, try using mind-mapping or doodling to kick-start some of your discussions. If your time is limited, you can choose to skip **Explore More** or split the whole session into two. Adapt the material in whatever way you think will help your group get the most out of God's word.

1

Our Father in Heaven
Matthew 6:5-9 and 7:7-11

The Big Idea
God is our heavenly Father: he loves to hear his children pray and he is able to answer our prayers.

Summary
Twice in Matthew 6:5-8 Jesus says, "When you pray, do not..." He highlights two ways that we are not to pray.

First, in verse 5 we are not to pray to impress other people. Those who do so receive a reward—people's admiration. But it's a reward from people rather than a reward from God. The test of whether we're really praying with God in view is whether we're as willing to pray in private as we are in public (v 6).

Second, in verse 7 we are not to pray to impress God. We can't manipulate God through our prayers. Lengthy prayers are not more likely to be answered. God knows what we need so we don't need to inform him (v 8).

The key is that in this section Jesus addresses God as Father and this is how he begins the Lord's Prayer. God is "our Father" who cares for us, so we don't need to manipulate him. And God is our Father "in heaven" so we can't manipulate him.

In Matthew 7:7-11 Jesus argues from the lesser to the greater. Most of the time human fathers give good gifts in response to the requests of their children. If we do

this, even though we are evil, how much more will our perfect heavenly Father be generous to us! These verses are a generous invitation to bring our requests to a caring Father.

Because we pray to our Father we can be confident that he will answer our prayers. Because our Father is in heaven we can be confident that he can answer our prayers.

Bear in mind that some people may have a difficult relationship with their human fathers and this may colour how they view their divine Father. Remind people that God is a good and perfect Father—the Father we long for. The very fact that earthly fathers sometimes disappoint us is because our expectations are instinctively shaped by the divine pattern of perfect fatherhood.

Optional Extra
Ask whether anyone has met a powerful person or a childhood hero. Ask how they felt about meeting that person. Did they feel overawed or diffident? Or invite people to consider the steps required for someone to speak with a monarch or president.

Then invite them to compare this with the steps required for a child of the monarch or president to approach them. It is hard for us to approach powerful people. But for most of us it is easy to talk with our parents. Link this example to the access we have to God, who is our Father, even though he is the most powerful person in the universe.

Guidance for Questions

1. **What words do you associate with the word "prayer"?**
   Ask people to shout out one-word responses. Don't correct or comment on people's responses (other than to encourage more responses).

• **What attitudes are revealed by those words?**
   There are no wrong answers to this question. It is an opportunity for people to express how they feel about prayer. There are likely to be a mix of responses—from pleasure and excitement to frustration and guilt.

2. **Twice in these verses Jesus says, "When you pray, do not..." What wrong ways to pray does Jesus identify?**
   In Matthew 6:5 we are not to pray to impress other people. In verse 7 we are not to pray to impress God (by our babbling).

3. **Why do the people Jesus describes pray this way?**
   The hypocrites' view of God is eclipsed by their desire to impress other people ("to be seen by others" in verse 5) so that in effect other people are more important to them than God. In verse 7, the babbling pagans seem to think that God needs to be won over by their commitment to prayer or that God can be manipulated (maybe even nagged) into giving them what they want (thinking they will be heard because of their many words). This in turn assumes they know better than God or that he needs to be persuaded to do what is best.

4. **How does the way that Jesus describes God serve to correct those wrong ways of praying?**
   We are often impressed by long prayers or stories of people praying for long periods of time. But in verses 5-6 Jesus warns us not to pray to impress other people. If we do then we receive our reward, but it is not a reward from God. If our motive is to relate to God rather than to impress others, our Father will reward us. In verse 8 Jesus says that God knows what we need. So we can pray short prayers! We don't need to explain the situation to him. And since God is our loving Father we don't need to persuade him to act. So short prayers can represent a trust in God's knowledge and care. (However, they can also sometimes reflect a lack of trust or delight in God if, for example, we don't pray much because we don't think prayer will make much difference.)

5. **When you pray as a group, how might you be tempted to pray:**
• **like the hypocrites Jesus describes in verse 5?**
   You may be tempted to pray long prayers or prayers full of Bible quotes

to impress other people. Or you might be reluctant to pray because you fear other people's disapproval if you say the wrong thing

- **like the babbling pagans of verse 7?** You might think that the longer you pray, the more likely it will be that God will answer. Or you might feel the need to explain to God what he should do and why.

6. How can you avoid doing so?

If prayer is not about impressing others, then we don't need to be eloquent or grammatically flawless when we pray aloud together. And if God knows what we need, then we can pray short prayers. We don't need to explain the situation to him. Sometimes it is helpful to agree together before you pray that you will just pray one-sentence prayers. This can be a helpful way of encouraging everyone to join in because they don't feel they have to impress the group or impress God by praying long and wordy prayers.

7. If God already knows what we need (as 6:8 says), why do you think Jesus encourages us to pray?

Prayer is not telling God what to do. It is not like putting money in a slot machine to get things out of God. We come as children to our Father to claim his promises. Prayer expresses our dependence on God and our trust in his care. So prayer deepens our relationship with God and allows us to contribute to his purposes.

8. What is the promise in verses 7-8?

This is not a promise that we can have whatever we want. The climax of this paragraph speaks of "good gifts", which means gifts that are for our spiritual good (v 11). God answers our prayers in his wisdom. He is not like an indulgent father handing out candy whenever his children ask. Nevertheless, there is a lovely encouragement here to bring our needs and longings to God. Remember, too, that our greatest good is to know God. So this is an invitation to seek God himself in prayer, knowing that we can have a real encounter with him through Christ.

9. What is Jesus' argument in verses 9-11?

Jesus is arguing from the lesser to the greater. If human fathers give good things in response to the requests of their children, how much more will the greatest Father, our Father in heaven? A stone looks a bit like a loaf of bread and a snake looks a bit like a fish. In this way, an evil father might enjoy playing cruel tricks on his children—handing them a stone and laughing at them when they try to bite into it. But God is not an evil father. He is the ultimate good Father who delights to give good gifts to his children.

10. How does this relationship with God as Father differ from the expectations of the hypocrites and babblers in Matthew 6:5-8?

At its heart, prayer is simply a child

talking to their Father. When Jesus invites us to pray "Our Father", he is inviting us to share the relationship with God that he has as God's Son. In Christ we are children of God with a Father who delights to hear our prayers. This is profoundly different from the prayers described in Matthew 6. If we know and love God as our Father, we will speak to him without caring about impressing anyone else. If we have confidence in his love for us as his children, we will not try to manipulate him or worry about whether or not he will hear us.

Explore More

o *Read Galatians 4:4-7. How does God the Son change our relationship with God?*
God sent his Son to redeem us and adopt us as his children. The Son ("born under the law") completes the legal process of our adoption.

o *How does God the Spirit change our relationship with God?*
God also sent the Spirit of the Son so we might experience our adoption. Paul describes the Spirit as "the Spirit of [the] Son" because he enables us to experience what the Son experiences—the love of the Father.

o *How does this affect our praying?*
This gives us confidence in prayer. Indeed, the very fact that we pray is a supernatural work of the Spirit. Most people are naturally diffident about approaching a monarch or president, *yet Christians routinely approach the King of the universe. We do this because of the Spirit's work in our hearts.*

---

11. **How will our prayers be shaped by knowing that God reigns from heaven?**
You could encourage people to explore how knowing that God reigns from heaven shapes both our attitude to prayer and the content of our prayers. We cannot manipulate God by our lengthy prayers. Because our Father is in heaven we can be confident he can answer our prayers.

12. **How will our prayers be shaped by knowing that God is our Father?**
You could encourage people to explore how knowing that God is our Father shapes both our attitude to prayer and the content of our prayers. We do not need to impress God or win him over because he loves us. Because we pray to our Father we can be confident that he will answer our prayers.

2

Hallowed Be Your Name

Matthew 1:18 – 2:12 and 28:16-20

The Big Idea

Jesus deserves to be worshipped, so we pray that we will worship him as we should and that others would join us in worshipping him.

- when we honour God with our lips and lives.
- through the mission of the church as other people join us in worshipping God.

Summary

"Hallowed" comes from the word "holy". God can't become more holy than he already is. So "hallowed be your name" is a prayer that God's name might be recognised as holy, or worshipped. In the Bible's worldview a person's name often summarises their character. So to hallow God's name is to honour God, especially the characteristics which are expressed in his names.

Matthew begins and ends his Gospel with Jesus receiving worship—from the Magi in Matthew 2 and from the disciples in Matthew 28. He also links this worship to the names of Jesus. Jesus is called "Jesus" (which means "the Lord saves") because "he will save his people from their sins" (1:21) and he is called "Immanuel" (which means "God with us") because God himself has come in the person of his Son (1:23).

Matthew's Gospel ends with Jesus sending us to call on the nations to submit to his name. We are to baptise people "in the name of the Father and of the Son and of the Holy Spirit" (28:19). God's name is hallowed…

Optional Extra

Before the meeting look up the meaning of everyone's name or the names of a few of those who will be attending. Books of names give their meanings or you can find the information online. Then read out the meaning and see if people know, or can guess, the name it describes. You could even decide whether the members of your group are aptly named! In this session we're going to discover that Jesus is aptly named and therefore his names summarise why we should honour him.

Guidance for Questions

1. Do you think your name suits you? Why, or why not?

We're going to be exploring how the names of Jesus express his identity and purpose. But most people's names are a bit more random. Sometimes people's personalities seem to match the sound or meaning of their name. Sometimes famous people shape the way we perceive a name.

2. What names will be given to the promised baby?

In Matthew 1:21 and 25 the baby is called "Jesus". In verse 23 the baby is called "Immanuel". (Questions 2 and 3 are simple text-based questions so do not linger on them.)

3. What do these names tell us about the baby?

"Jesus" means "the Lord saves". Jesus "will save his people from their sins" (v 21). "Immanuel" means "God with us" (v 23). Jesus is God and is God-made-man living among his people.

4. Why have the Magi come to find Jesus? What do they do when they find him?

The Magi have come to worship Jesus (v 2). When they find Jesus, they worship him and honour him with gifts (v 11).

5. Why does Herod say he wants to find Jesus?

In verse 8 Herod claims he wants to worship Jesus.

• What light does verse 12 shed on that?

He has no intention of worshipping Jesus. The Magi are warned in a dream that Herod is a threat to Jesus. (Look forward to verse 16 to see Herod's real bloody intentions.)

6. If we started with worship more often, how do you think the rest of our prayers would change?

A lot can be revealed in the way we pray. In the first session we saw that if you view God as your Father then you will not feel the need to manipulate him through long prayers. Here we find that our prayers can reveal our true priorities. Are we living for God's glory or for our own comfort? This is not just about whether we praise God or petition God. It is also about how we petition God. We can ask God to meet our needs in a way that will lead to his name being hallowed. Don't assume worship is absent from people's prayers. Many people in your group may often include worship in their prayers. If so, this is an opportunity to affirm and encourage them.

7. What do the disciples do when they see the risen Jesus?

Look at verse 17. The disciples worship Jesus when they see him (though some also continue to doubt). This is a simple question with one clear answer so do not try to develop this into a lengthy discussion. The aim is simply to make the connection back to Matthew 2. If people do not make this connection then you can ask, "What is the link with the story of the Magi?"

8. What reasons are there to worship Jesus in these verses?

Jesus is the one who has been given all authority (v 18) and therefore he is to be obeyed (v 20). Jesus is also named with the Father and the Spirit which suggests he is God.

9. What will those who worship him do?

The eleven disciples of verse 16, who are also the worshippers of verse 17, are to make more disciples and more worshippers.

10. What does that have to do with God's name?

In the Bible a person's name often summarises or represents their character. To worship God is to recognise that his name is worthy. This is what it means to hallow his name.

Explore More

o **Read Matthew 15:1-9. Where did the Pharisees go wrong?**

The Pharisees appeared very religious. Indeed, in verse 2 they question the lack of commitment displayed by the disciples of Jesus. But Jesus says all their religious rules are actually a way of toning down the radical call to love God and others (v 3-6). Their religious rules defined what was "just enough" rather than describing a whole-hearted response to God's love.

o **How might we fall into the trap of honouring God's name with our lips but not with our lives?**

These verses are a call to ensure that the enthusiasm we feel in corporate worship is matched by a similar enthusiasm for glorifying God's name through everyday obedience. Encourage the group to think specifically about things they say in church which are not reflected in their daily lives.

---

11. Think about your church: what would it mean to pray for God's name to be hallowed there?

Encourage people to identify specific ways in which you could pray that you all as a group or as a church will honour God with both your lips and your lives.

12. Think about your neighbourhood and your country: how can you pray for God's name to be hallowed there?

Encourage people to identify specific ways in which you could pray for more people to become worshippers of Jesus.

3

Your Kingdom Come
Matthew 13:1-23 and 13:31-32

The Big Idea

God's kingdom comes now through the proclamation of the word and will come in glory when Christ returns, so we pray for the mission of the church and the return of Christ.

Summary

The kingdom of heaven is good news (Matthew 4:23). It is good news because the kingdom of heaven is the restoration of God's rule of peace, plenty and protection. This was what the rule of God was like before humanity rejected God's rule, and it is what it will be like when Christ returns.

The problem is that the kingdom of heaven is not good news for those who have rebelled against that rule—and that includes all of humanity. So the kingdom comes in two stages. First, it comes in grace with God's call to repentance and the offer of forgiveness in Christ. Second, it comes in glory and judgment when Christ returns.

Taken together, the parables of the kingdom in Matthew 13 elaborate on this two-stage coming. Jesus is saying:

- just because the kingdom of God has not come in glory does not mean it has not come at all in the present—it has come first in a gracious, secret way as the word is proclaimed.
- just because the kingdom of God has

come in a gracious, secret way does not mean it will not come in glory in the future—it will come in glory when Christ returns.

So to pray "Your kingdom come" is to pray that…

- in the present the word would be proclaimed and people would respond with faith.
- in the future Christ will return to restore God's reign of peace and plenty.

The coming of the kingdom of heaven also challenges our priorities. We are to seek first God's kingdom by obeying his word and proclaiming his word.

Optional Extra

Invite people to think back to the last time they read a newspaper or watched the news on the television or online. Ask them, "What evidence did you come across to suggest that Jesus is Lord and that humanity is living under his rule?" You could bring a newspaper and hand out sections of it to people so they can search for themselves. For the most part the evidence will be thin on the ground. This world does not yet appear to be under the rule of Christ and most of humanity does not live in obedience to his rule. This exercise is designed to get people thinking about what it means to say the kingdom is present now and is coming in the future, along with what it means to pray for it to come—issues addressed in the passage we will be looking at.

Guidance for Questions

1. **"On Sunday morning I sing about Jesus being King, but on Monday morning I only get grief from my colleagues if I speak about Jesus to them." Do you ever experience a gap like this between Sunday and Monday morning? Why is this?**
This question aims to introduce the idea that the kingdom of heaven/ of God is not yet a universal reality, but neither is it wholly absent. The kingdom of heaven has come in some ways and not in other ways.

2. **How does the kingdom of heaven grow within history?**
Look at verse 23. The kingdom grows when people hear God's word and respond positively with fruit-bearing faith. Those who respond positively become part of the kingdom and bear fruit so the kingdom grows.

• **You could also read verses 10-17. What light do these verses shed on this question?**
   • v 11-13: those who receive the kingdom by faith will be rewarded while those who reject the kingdom through unbelief will be rejected.
   • v 16-17: not everyone sees the kingdom so not everyone responds positively to the word with faith.
   • v 14-15: this is God's judgment on those who continue to reject him.

3. **In what negative ways do people respond to the message of Jesus?**
The four soils represent four responses.
   • Soil #1 (v 4, 19): Some people hear the word and they immediately dismiss it because Satan has taken it from them.
   • Soil #2 (v 5-6, 20-21): Some people initially respond well, but it is not true faith so they fall away when things get hard.
   • Soil #3 (v 7, 22): Some people are distracted by worries or wealth. Their faith is choked.

4. **In what positive ways do people respond to the message of Jesus?**
Soil #4 (v 8, 23): The good soil represents those who respond with faith and produce fruit.

5. **How does Jesus apply this parable? What command does he give (v 9)?**
The one command in this passage is "Whoever has ears, let them hear". Jesus calls on us to hear the message of the kingdom and accept God's kingship. This is the way to enjoy the blessing of God's kingdom (v 16). Jesus is speaking to "large crowds" (v 2) so he is concerned that they listen with genuine intent and not just to be entertained. Through his preaching he is distinguishing between those who are in the kingdom (who know its secrets, as verses 11-12 put it) and those who are not (v 13-15).

6. **How would you summarise "the message about the kingdom" (v 19) in your own words?**

God is the rightful King of the world. He is restoring his reign through Jesus. God graciously invites us to turn from our rebellion and find blessing under his rule. One day Jesus will return and God's reign will be undisputed (Philippians 2:10-11). Those who have submitted to Jesus will be rewarded while those who continued to reject him will be judged.

Explore More

○ *Read Matthew 27:41-42. How did the religious leaders challenge Jesus to prove he is God's promised King?*

The religious leaders think Jesus can prove he is God's promised King by coming down from the cross and therefore saving himself.

○ *What did Jesus do instead?*

Jesus proves he is God's promised King by staying on the cross and therefore saving others.

7. **Jesus applies this parable by commanding us to hear (v 9). Who do you know who has not yet heard about Jesus? How could you make sure they get the chance to hear and respond?**

You could split the group into smaller pairs or threes to discuss specific ways in which they could bring the message of the gospel to those they know.

8. **What does this image tell us about the kingdom of heaven in the present?**

The kingdom of heaven is like a mustard seed—the smallest of all seeds. In the present the kingdom is largely unnoticed. Most people around us do not submit to God and are unaware of his reign.

9. **What does it tell us about the kingdom of heaven in the future?**

The kingdom of heaven grows and will keep growing. Many people find refuge under Christ's rule (like birds perching in the branches of a tree). When Christ returns, the kingdom of heaven will fill the earth. Christ will return in glory, and everyone will acknowledge that he is King.

10. **In what ways do you think this future has already begun to happen?**

The process of gathering people into the kingdom of heaven is taking place through the mission of the church.

Explore More

○ *Read 2 Peter 3:3-9. How does Peter counter the accusation that the kingdom of God is never going to come in judgment? What reason does he give for the delay?*

First, we can be sure that God will judge the earth because there is a precedent—the flood during the time of Noah (v 5-7). Second, what feels like a long delay to us is not a long delay from the perspective of eternity (v 8). The reason for the delay is to give people time to repent (v 9). So the delay is actually a sign of God's patience.

○ **Read 2 Peter 3:10-13. What will the fulfilment of God's kingdom look like?**
The coming of God's kingdom involves judgment: everything being "laid bare" (v 10) for all to see. The world as we know it will be destroyed. But God promises a new and better world: one where we will be with God for ever and where "righteousness dwells" (v 13).

---

11. **What specific things could you pray about when you ask for God's kingdom to come:**
• **in the present?**
We can pray that God's word would be proclaimed and that people would respond with fruit-bearing faith. You could ask people to identify specific examples of this—like praying for opportunities with unbelieving friends, evangelistic initiatives in your church or for missionaries supported by your church. You can use your answers to this question in the prayer time.

• **in the future?**
Ultimately we are praying for Christ to return and restore God's reign of peace and plenty.

12. **How should the coming of the kingdom in the future shape our attitude to the kingdom in the present?**
If this world is all there is, then it makes sense to live for the treasures of this world. But we believe the kingdom of heaven is coming in glory when Christ returns, so it makes sense to prioritise God's kingdom in the present. For those who have not turned to Christ in faith, the coming of the kingdom will mean judgment, so its coming is also a powerful incentive for evangelism.

4

Your Will Be Done
Matthew 26:36-46

The Big Idea

This is a prayer that we might submit to God's will just as Jesus did: accepting that God's intentions are best, and putting him first in all we do.

Summary

The Bible speaks of God's will in two senses:

- God's sovereign will: everything that happens is part of God's sovereign will since he is in control of everything.
- God's moral will: the attitudes and behaviours that please God and which are revealed in the Bible.

When we pray "your will be done" we are praying that people (including us) might follow God's moral will. But we are also praying that we might submit to God's sovereign will. We know this because Matthew uses exactly the same phrase in his account of Jesus in Gethsemane where Jesus expresses his submission to God's will—even though it will cost him everything (26:42).

For some people in your group, submitting to God's sovereign will may feel hard because they are going through a difficult time. Christians may be called to accept suffering as Jesus did. But there is also something unique about the sufferings of Jesus. Matthew 26:42 reminds us that Jesus drank the cup of God's wrath so we

don't have to. This means that, whatever happens to us in this life, we are free from judgment and heading for glory. It also means we can be confident that God's intentions towards us are good.

Optional Extra

If you have someone in your group who has suffered and suffered well (perhaps through ill-health, bereavement or unemployment), ask them beforehand if they would be willing to speak about that experience or be interviewed. Invite them to talk about how it felt, what it meant to trust God in suffering, what it meant for them to submit to God's will and what part prayer played in helping them respond well to their problems.

You could include this at the beginning or end of your study.

Guidance for Questions

1. **How do children react when they don't get their own way? How do adults react?**

   The aim of this question is to introduce the idea of submitting to someone else's will, even when that is not what we want. People may find it easier to talk about children and their reactions. But you may discover that adult reactions are simply a more sophisticated version of children's reactions.

People may share personal stories at this point, but do not push this if people are reluctant to disclose in this way.

2. How does Matthew describe the emotions of Jesus in these verses?
Look at verse 37 which says Jesus began to be "sorrowful and troubled". Look at verse 38 where Jesus says, "My soul is overwhelmed with sorrow to the point of death".

3. Why is Jesus feeling these emotions?
Look at verse 45. Jesus knows that the time has come for him to suffer and die. He knows he is about to be betrayed, arrested, deserted, slandered, mis-tried, condemned, beaten, flogged, mocked, crucified and forsaken by his Father as he bears the judgment for human sin.

4. What does Jesus request in his prayer of verse 39?
Jesus asks for the cup of suffering (on the cross) to be taken from him. Often in the Old Testament, draining a cup is a picture of receiving the judgment of God. (See, for example, Psalm 75:7-8; Isaiah 51:17; Jeremiah 25:15-16.)

• What difference do you think it made to add "Yet not as I will, but as you will"?
First, allow the group to think back to their previous answers and consider what difference it made to the way Jesus felt. Second, think about how God answers this prayer. The external circumstances do not change—the cross remains before Jesus. The will of the Father does not change. But Jesus has come to a point of submission to the will of God—despite the cost. Look, for example, at verses 51-54 where Jesus rejects both human and angelic interventions that might prevent the cross because the cross is the plan of God promised in the Scriptures.

5. What is the difference between the prayers in verse 39 and verse 42?
Verse 39 begins "If it is possible" as if the possibility is open. But verse 42 begins "If it is not possible" because the possibility is closed. Verse 39 is a request qualified by a declaration of submission. Verse 42 is simply a declaration of submission. Praying "your will be done" has enabled Jesus to understand and submit to the Father's will.

6. How does the story of Gethsemane help us to see what it means for us to pray this?
For Jesus to pray "your will be done" in 26:42 was an act of submission to God's will. For us to pray "your will be done" in 6:10 is also an act of submission to God's will. Seeing the way Jesus felt as he prayed shows us that this is a prayer we are likely to find difficult. But forcing ourselves to pray it is often the first step towards actually meaning it and living it out. Like Jesus, we should be confident that God's will can be trusted and is best. Romans 8:28 tells us that "in all things

God works for the good of those who love him".

7. When things don't go our way, how might we behave if we are not submitting to God's sovereign will?

We might become bitter and resentful towards God. Or we might become frantic or aggressive as we try to take control of our lives. Or we might think that, since God is not delivering what we want, we are justified in breaking his moral will.

8. What attitude do you need in order to start a prayer with these requests?

The first three requests in the Lord's Prayer reflect an attitude of submission to God's will and trust in him. People who put God first will pray these prayers. At the same time, one reason it is helpful to have these words provided for us by Jesus is that they will help us to put God first when we struggle to do so. We can pray these prayers as a way of asking God to help us to submit to him and put him first.

9. How does the phrase "as it is in heaven" alter the way you think about these requests?

"On earth as it is in heaven" may refer to all the first three petitions ("hallowed be your name", "your kingdom come", "your will be done") or just to "your will be done". It reminds us that there is a place where God's name is already hallowed, his reign is already acknowledged and his will is already done. Jesus ascended through the clouds to receive the worship of heaven and to be given all authority. On earth his reign is contested and his will is resisted, but in heaven he is acclaimed as Lord. Yet the authority which Jesus received in heaven was authority over both heaven and earth (Matthew 28:18). So heaven is a sign and reminder of the future of this earth when Jesus returns.

10. How is praying "your will be done" similar to praying "hallowed be your name" and "your kingdom come"? How is it different?

- All three petitions have a present and future dimension. We are praying for God's name to be honoured, his kingdom to come and his will to be done in the present through the mission of the church. And we are also praying for the return of Christ.

- All three petitions have a personal and missional dimension. We pray as individuals for our holiness—that in our lives we might honour God's name, submit to his reign and obey his will. And we are also praying for missional advance so that more people worship Christ, and for his kingdom to grow as people submit to his reign and obey his will.

- It's actually harder to discern the differences between these petitions, for they offer different perspectives on the same reality. But the use of similar language in the rest of Matthew's Gospel suggests the focus of "your kingdom come" might be more on mission (Matthew 13:1-23; 28:18-20) while the focus of "your will be done" might be more on holiness and submission (Matthew 26:36-44).

Explore More

○ **Read 1 Peter 2:21-25. How does the submission of Jesus help us?**
Jesus is our example and inspiration (v 21). An example alone can be intimidating, especially when we find it hard to measure up to. But Jesus' sufferings are unique: we will not have to suffer as greatly as him. He drank the cup of God's wrath so we don't have to, bearing our sins for us (v 24). This enables us to "live for righteousness", since by his Spirit Jesus helps us to obey and submit to God. Jesus is also described as our "Shepherd and Overseer" (v 25). He is always with us to guide us.

All this means that, whatever happens to us in this life, we are free from judgment and heading for glory. It also shows us that God's intentions towards us are good, even if we can't understand what God is doing in a particular situation, because he gave his Son for us on the cross.

---

11. In what areas of life do you find it hard to put God first? Why?
The instinct of our old selves is to put ourselves first. We may do this in prayer (e.g. starting with our own requests); in church (e.g. prioritising our own preferences and tastes); in our work (e.g. failing to share Jesus with our colleagues); with our finances (e.g. keeping all our income for ourselves rather than sharing with the needy); and in our home life (e.g. failing to be hospitable to outsiders). Sometimes this is because we are afraid of others or of the future; sometimes it is because we simply don't think carefully about our priorities. Sometimes putting God first will be genuinely costly, but it will always be worth it.

12. How could we remind ourselves to put God first?
Spending time reading the Bible and in prayer, both alone and with other Christians, will help us to reset our priorities. This is not just something which must be done by our own efforts: it is something God helps us with. We will all fail to put God first, but by faith in Jesus we will be forgiven, and by his Spirit we will be helped to keep going.

5

Give Us Today Our Daily Bread

Matthew 6:25-34

The Big Idea

Our heavenly Father cares for us, so we can bring our worries to him in prayer and be free to put his kingdom first rather than focusing on our own needs.

Summary

Jesus begins and ends Matthew 6:25-34 by telling us not to worry. In between he gives us a number of reasons why we need not worry.

- What we worry about is often not as important as we think (v 25).
- Worry serves no useful purpose (v 27).
- The world around us shows that God cares for what he has made (v 26, 28-29).
- God especially cares for his children (v 26, 30).

The root issue is "little faith" (v 30). Jesus describes God as "your heavenly Father" in verses 26 and 32. God is able and willing to care for his children. Therefore we can have faith in him.

This brings us back to the Lord's Prayer, which begins "Our Father in heaven".

To pray "give us today our daily bread" is...

- to ask our Father to provide for his children as he has promised to do.
- to bring our worries to him so we no longer carry them.

Bringing our needs to our Father and trusting his care frees us to seek first his kingdom (v 32-33). "Give us today our daily bread" is not a licence to indulge our whims—asking God for whatever we'd like right now. We pray this prayer so that, free from worry, we can focus our time, money and energy on the kingdom of God.

Optional Extra

Make a list of phobias. Shout out the names and see if people know (or can guess) what they are the fear of. Here are some examples. Ablutophobia = the fear of washing. Acrophobia = the fear of heights. Arachnophobia = the fear of spiders. Claustrophobia = the fear of confined spaces. Dentophobia = the fear of dentists. Hemophobia = the fear of blood.

Guidance for Questions

1. **What do you worry about?**

   Try to encourage the group to be honest about their worries—big or small. If there is time you could also ask them to talk about how that worry affects them.

2. **Jesus repeatedly tells us not to worry in these verses. What reason**

does he give for not worrying:

- **in verse 25?**

  "Is not life more than food, and the body more than clothes?" If people simply repeat this question, ask them what it means. It suggests that many of the things we worry about are not as important as we think they are—certainly not when viewed from the perspective of eternity.

- **in verse 27?**

  Worrying doesn't achieve anything. Indeed, it sometimes makes things worse. You could follow this up by asking people for examples of times when worrying has been futile or even counter-productive.

3. **Look at verse 30. What is the root cause of worry?**

   Jesus says those who worry have "little faith". Ask people how a lack of faith leads to a load of worry.

4. **What does Jesus tell us to do in verses 26 and 28? How does this help counter worry?**

   Jesus tells us to look at the birds in verse 26 and at the flowers in verse 28. The world around us is full of evidence of our Father's care. We live in a fathered world. Jesus then argues from the lesser to the greater in verses 26 and 30: if God cares for birds and flowers, then how much more will he care for his children? Don't miss the command in these verses. This is a command to look and learn from the world around us—to see God at work in the natural world.

5. **Have you had experiences of looking at the world around you and being filled with wonder or re-assured of God's care?**

   This is an opportunity to share fun facts about the world or favourite observations. The point is to reinforce the idea that this is a fathered world cared for by our heavenly Father.

6. **How does Jesus describe God in these verses?**

   Twice Jesus describes God as "your heavenly Father" (v 26, 32). This is how the Lord's Prayer begins: "Our Father in heaven". We have a heavenly Father who cares for us. If people do not make the connection you could ask, "Where have we met this idea before in our studies?"

- **Reflect on each word of this phrase. How does it help us even more?**

  "Your" = God is connected to you and committed to you through Christ. "Heavenly" = God is powerful enough to provide for your needs. "Father" = God loves you and cares for you. Reflecting on this phrase reminds us of all these reasons not to worry.

Explore More

○ **Read Matthew 14:13-21. What lesson should the disciples have learned from this story?**

  The disciples should have seen that Jesus is a compassionate King (v 14) who provides for his people (v 20).

○ *Read verses 22-26. How did they react the next time they were in trouble?*

"Immediately" after the feeding of the 5,000 (v 22) they are "terrified" when they see Jesus coming to their aid (v 26). The root problem is exactly the same as it was in chapter 6. In both 6:30 and 14:31 Jesus says, "You of little faith".

○ *Read verses 27-33. How did Peter show faith? What caused him to stop having faith?*

Peter does show faith in that he believes that it is Jesus and even walks out to him on the water (v 29). But quickly he becomes afraid because of the wind (v 30). Even though he clearly knows he can trust Jesus, he doesn't manage to do so.

---

7. **In what ways does the prayer "give us today our daily bread" express the attitude that Jesus is telling us to have in Matthew 6:25?**

Praying "Give us today our daily bread" in the context of a prayer which begins "Our Father in heaven" reminds us that we have a Father who can care and does care. We can hand our concerns to our heavenly Father so we no longer carry them.

8. **According to Jesus, what is to be our priority?**

Look at verse 33. We are to seek first the kingdom of God and his righteousness.

9. **What distracts us from this priority?**

Sometimes we worry because we fear we will lack things ("What shall we eat?"), and sometimes because we are desperate to gain more ("pagans run after all these things"). It is striking that Jesus tells us that both these types of worry are foolish. They prevent us from making the kingdom of God our priority.

10. **What do we need to remind ourselves of in order not to be distracted?**

Look at verse 32. God knows what we need so we do not need to concern ourselves with these worries. Look at verse 33. God is able and willing to provide the things we need. We can trust him to look after us and to know what is best for us.

11. **What might it look like in practice for us to make the kingdom of God our priority?**

Making the kingdom our priority means submitting to the rule of God by obeying his word (seeking "his righteousness"). When we looked at the parable of the sower in Matthew 13 we saw that the kingdom grows as the word is proclaimed. So making the kingdom of God our priority also means proclaiming the word of God that other people might submit to the rule of God.

12. **When we pray "Give us today our daily bread", what are we asking for?**

There is no need to make this

complicated: we are praying for God to provide our needs. In the context of Matthew 6, this is the cry of a child to their father. You could ask people to spot the references to "your Father" in Matthew 6 (v 1, 4, 6 (x2), 8, 9, 14, 15, 18 (x2), 26, 32). We are asking our Father to be true to his promises and look after his children.

- **How does that help us to have the right priorities?**

Bringing our needs to our Father and trusting his care frees us to seek first his kingdom (v 32-33). "Give us today our daily bread" is not a licence to indulge our whims—asking God for whatever we'd like right now. We pray this prayer so that, free from worry, we can focus our time, money and energy on the kingdom of God.

6

Forgive Us Our Sins
Matthew 9:1-8 and 18:21-35

The Big Idea

Asking for forgiveness and receiving forgiveness reassures us of God's grace and prompts us to be merciful.

Summary

In Matthew 9 a paralysed man is brought to Jesus. But instead of healing him, Jesus declares that his sins are forgiven. It is a sign that forgiveness is our number one need—even more than physical health. The religious leaders are scandalised because only God can forgive sin. But Jesus proves he has the authority to forgive by healing the man. This gives us the confidence to ask for forgiveness in the Lord's Prayer.

Asking for forgiveness (even though we are already forgiven) prompts us to repent, reminds us that we need God's mercy and reassures us of God's grace.

The Lord's Prayer links receiving forgiveness with showing forgiveness: "And forgive us our debts, as we also have forgiven our debtors." Jesus expands on this line in Matthew 6:14-15: "For if you forgive other people when they sin against you, your heavenly Father will also forgive you. But if you do not forgive others their sins, your Father will not forgive your sins."

At first sight this appears to imply that we earn forgiveness by being forgiving. But God's forgiveness comes first. Showing forgiveness is not the reason for our forgiveness by God; instead showing forgiveness is the evidence of our forgiveness by God. This is what we see in the parable Jesus tells in Matthew 18:21-35. The master's forgiveness comes first. But the servant does not live as someone who has received forgiveness.

The Lord's Prayer speaks not of "sin", but of "debts". Debt is a powerful picture for sin, because sin is failing to meet our obligations towards God: we lack the resources to repay what we owe. But cancelling debt is also an allusion to Deuteronomy 15:1. This link suggests that forgiving debts in the Lord's Prayer is also a call to be merciful and generous in all our relationships.

Optional Extra

Use the internet to find the results of surveys in which people are asked what they consider the biggest problems to be in their neighbourhood or nation. Read out the findings and ask people to guess the order in which they come. You could even throw in a few red herrings to make it more fun! In Matthew 9 we are going to discover that humanity's biggest need is not what most people think it is.

Guidance for Questions

1. **When was the last time someone forgave you? What did it feel like?**

   In this session we're going to think about the joy of being forgiven. But we're also going to think about how being forgiven is life-changing because it makes us merciful people. People may be reluctant to tell stories of major failings for which they've re-

ceived forgiveness. That's fine. Don't push people to divulge more than they want to. Any example will illustrate the joy-giving, life-changing nature of being forgiven.

2. **What is the immediate need of the man who is brought to Jesus? What is the ultimate need of the man?**

   Look at Matthew 9:2. The man is paralysed. His friends hope Jesus will heal him of his physical infirmity. But Jesus says, "Your sins are forgiven". Jesus addresses his spiritual plight because this man's ultimate need (like all of us) is forgiveness.

3. **What does his response to the man make us think of Jesus?**

   Modern readers are often surprised by the way Jesus ignores the man's physical infirmity, because our culture focuses on physical needs and material blessings. But in verse 3, those who were there were shocked by the claim that Jesus could forgive sins. They knew that only God could forgive sin. So they regarded the words of Jesus as blasphemous—which they would be if Jesus was not Immanuel, God with us (Matthew 1:23). Jesus proves he has the authority to forgive by healing the man. This gives us the confidence to ask for forgiveness ourselves.

4. **How does Jesus respond to the religious leaders?**

   Look at verses 4-7. Jesus says their response is evil. That's because they are denying that Jesus can forgive sins and therefore dissuading people from receiving forgiveness through Jesus. Jesus then proves he has the authority to forgive by healing the man. Sickness first entered the good world God had made as part of the curse on human sin. Jesus proves he can deal with the root problem (sin) by dealing with one of the symptoms (sickness).

5. Do you think the crowd are right in the way they respond to Jesus?

"Filled with awe" in verse 8 is literally "filled with fear". In some ways this is a right response because someone with the power to forgive holds our eternal future in his hands. It is also right to praise God because forgiveness is available through Christ. But the crowd stop short of recognising the full implications of what has just happened. They recognise that Jesus is a man with authority, but they do not recognise that he is God.

6. If you're a Christian then all your sins—past, present and future—are forgiven through the cross. So why does Jesus encourage us to continue to pray "forgive us our sins"?

Regularly praying for forgiveness (as Jesus instructs us to do in the Lord's Prayer)…

- prompts us to review our lives and repent of our sin.
- reminds us that we are sinners who are dependent on God's mercy.
- restores our assurance of forgiveness.
- renews our sense of living in relationship with God.

But it is important to know that our sin does not break our relationship, not even temporarily. God's mercy does not fluctuate or depend on our performance. We are not out of relationship with God until we ask for forgiveness. Indeed, it is because we are accepted by grace that we can have the confidence to come to him and confess our sins. If people are struggling with this question you could ask, "What is the effect on us of asking God for forgiveness?"

7. Think about what the different elements of the story represent. What is Jesus telling us about…

- **what sin is like?**

Our sin is like a debt that we owe to God. That's how sin is described in the Lord's Prayer (Matthew 6:12). We have obligations towards our Creator and King—to love him, worship him and obey him. But we have failed to meet those obligations. What's more, we have no resources to catch up on the payments or repay the debt.

- **what is happening when God has mercy?**

God in his mercy cancels the debt of those who come to him in faith.

8. How should the king's forgiveness make the servant feel about himself?

The servant should feel deeply grateful, realising that he had nothing to offer and deserved punishment. He should have a humbler outlook and an attitude of total devotion to the king who has shown mercy to him.

- **Does it actually have that effect (v 28-30)?**

  The servant has no appreciation of the forgiveness he has received. He does not live as a forgiven man. He acts as though he is better than the other servant, even though his debt was actually greater. He insists on the letter of the law—even though he himself cannot live by the letter of the law.

9. **How do the other people in the story react to the servant's refusal to forgive?**

   Look at verse 31. The other servants are "outraged" by his refusal to forgive. Look at verses 32-33. The master describes him as "wicked". Look at verse 34. The master imprisons him. This sentence is effectively imprisonment for ever, since the servant has no resources to repay his debt.

10. **According to the story, which comes first—our mercy or God's mercy? What is the evidence that we have received forgiveness from God?**

    In the story the mercy of the king comes before the lack of mercy from the servant. It's the same with our salvation. God's forgiveness comes first. If we have truly received mercy then we will show mercy. So the evidence that we have truly received forgiveness from God is that we show forgiveness to others.

Explore More

- **Read Deuteronomy 15:1-15. What does God tell his people to do in verses 1, 10, 11 and 12?**

  God tells his people to cancel debts, give generously, be open-handed and free slaves.

- **What reason does God give for these commands in verse 15?**

  They are to be generous because they know what it is like to be enslaved and they know what it is like to receive mercy.

- **How does this help us to understand what it means to pray this line of the Lord's Prayer?**

  The links with Deuteronomy 15 suggest that forgiving debts in the Lord's Prayer means more than overlooking personal wrongs. We are to be a liberating community because we have been liberated from sin. We are to be generous people because God has been generous to us. (To explore this more, look up Acts 4:33-35 and notice the link with Deuteronomy 15:4.) This prayer changes those who truly pray it!

11. **How can we reflect God's mercy in the way we treat other people?**

    In the context of the Lord's Prayer the primary way we reflect the mercy we have received is by forgiving other people. Encourage the group to identify practical examples of this. But the link to Deuteronomy 15:1

(see Explore More above) suggests a wider application. We should be open-handed people because God has been generous to us.

12. **What kind of person are we asking God to make us into when we pray, "Forgive us our sins as we forgive those who sin against us"?**

The Lord's Prayer is a reminder that we need forgiveness and that we have received forgiveness from God through Christ. It should therefore make us grateful and merciful people. Praying this line is a regular prompt to forgive those who have wronged us and to be reconciled with those with whom we have fallen out. It should produce healthy relationships, families and churches.

7

Lead Us Not Into Temptation
Matthew 4:1-11 and 26:40-41

The Big Idea
Though failure is never final for Christians, we can fail when tested and fall when tempted, so we pray for deliverance from evil.

Summary
The word "temptation" literally means "testing" and describes a broad range of trials, not just being enticed to sin (though it can include being enticed to sin, as Matthew 4:1 indicates). Elsewhere the Bible tells us to rejoice when we face "trials" (James 1:2-3). So we are praying here to be delivered not in the sense of being spared trials, but in the sense of spared from sinning or giving up when we are tested (delivered "out from" or "through" temptation).

Matthew 4 uses the same language as the Lord's Prayer to speak of Jesus being tempted or tested in the wilderness for 40 days. Jesus counters these temptations by quoting the words of Scripture. The truth of God's word counters the lies of Satan's temptations.

In Matthew 26 Peter confidently declares that he will not "fall" even though Jesus has predicted that he will (26:33-35). Then Peter is tested three times (like Jesus in Matthew 4) and fails three times (unlike Jesus) (26:69-75). In between these two events, Jesus tells Peter: "Watch and pray so that you will not fall into temptation" (26:41). It is a phrase that echoes the final line of the Lord's Prayer (6:13). Peter falls because he relies on himself too much and so does not turn to God in prayer. The prayer he should have prayed is, "Lead us not into temptation, but deliver us from the evil one" (6:13).

In the wilderness, Jesus is replaying the story of humanity and the story of Israel. Adam fell when he was tempted by Satan whereas Jesus remains faithful. Israel failed when tested during their 40 years in the wilderness whereas Jesus remains faithful during his 40 days in the wilderness.

So Jesus is not simply giving an example to follow. Just as Adam was the representative of humanity, so Jesus is the representative of the new humanity, his people. So for Christians, failure is never final because Jesus has passed the test on our behalf.

Optional Extra

Announce that you are going to start with a quiz. Then make all the questions impossibly hard, either because they involve obscure pieces of knowledge (like "What is the fifth largest city in Uzbekistan?") or the answers are personal (like "What did I have for lunch today?"). Or you could choose questions that can easily be answered by some people but are impossible for others. This session is going to focus on what it's like to be tested, including what it's like to fail.

Guidance for Questions

1. **What has been your worst exam experience? What does it feel like to fail a test?**
   In this session we're going to explore the challenge of being tested as

Christians. But we will find comfort in knowing that Jesus has passed the test and through his faithfulness his people have all passed the "entrance exam" required to enter God's kingdom. This question should be a light exercise as people look back or share funny stories. But if an exam failure is still a raw experience for someone then this study should encourage them because we will see the approval and acceptance that we have in Christ.

2. **What similarities are there between these verses?**
   Both verses talk about being "led", about being "tempted", and about "Satan" or "the evil one".

3. **What temptations does Jesus face?**
   Don't spend too long on this question. It would be possible to debate the exact nature of each temptation at length. But to understand the Lord's Prayer it is enough for people to engage with the reality that Jesus was tempted.

   - v 3: Satan tempts Jesus to use the rights of divine sonship, which he had set aside to complete his mission of saving the lost (Philippians 2:6).
   - v 5-6: Satan tempts Jesus to prove his divine sonship in a way that manipulates God.
   - v 8-9: Satan tempts Jesus to shortcut the cross and therefore the redemption of his people while leaving Satan's authority intact.

4. How does Jesus overcome these temptations?

Each time Jesus resists temptation, he does so by quoting God's word. Each time he says, "It is written …" (v 4, 7, 10). It may also be that the 40 days of fasting described in verse 2 were a preparation for the testing that was about to come.

Explore More

o *Read 1 Corinthians 10:13. What does this verse say about temptation?*

Everyone is tempted—it is the common experience of mankind. But this verse promises that God will provide "a way out" of temptation. In other words, we do not face temptation alone. God is with us through his Spirit to help us stand firm. Often, in the midst of temptation, the Spirit reminds us of the truth. Or the opportunity to sin stalls, requiring more of a conscious decision to continue. It is as if God is opening up an exit route for us in these moments.

o *How does it help us understand what it means to pray, "Lead us not into temptation, but deliver us from the evil one"?*

The Lord's Prayer cannot be asking for us to be spared temptation. Instead we are praying for God to be true to his promise to provide a way out. We are also praying that we will have the wisdom to spot the way out and the will to take it.

5. What would have helped Peter not to fail when tested and fall when tempted?

Jesus calls on Peter to "watch and pray". The exhortation comes in between Peter's overconfident declaration that he will not "fall" (26:33) and his three denials of Jesus. The implication is that Peter's fall could have been avoided if he had prayed. The prayer Peter should have prayed is in the Lord's Prayer: "Lead us not into temptation, but deliver us from the evil one".

6. Why do you think he didn't do as he was told (but slept instead, v 43)?

The problem is not just that Peter did not pray (which might imply prayer is a magic formula against failure). The problem is that Peter was too confident in himself, as his rejection of Jesus' warning in 26:34-35 reveals. He does not pray because he trusts in himself and this is why he fails.

7. What key ways of resisting temptation have we seen?

We, too, ought to "watch and pray" (26:41). If we are to avoid failing when tested or falling when tempted then we must pray the Lord's Prayer: "Lead us not into temptation, but deliver us from the evil one". We are not to be confident in our own ability to remain faithful. Instead, we should look to God for help and the way we do this is through prayer.

We can also, like Jesus, use the Scriptures to help us to look to God.

The Bible will tell us the truth about God and help us to resist the evil one. Memorising Bible verses will help us to have such truths ready for testing times.

- **Are these the things we usually do when we face testing times, or do we try other things instead?**

  This is a reflection question designed to help the group think practically about their own response to temptation. It could be helpful to think of a specific time they have been tempted in the past. How could watching, praying and reading the Bible have helped them?

8. **Look again at Matthew 4:1 and 6:13. How does what happened to Jesus differ from what we are told to pray for ourselves?**

   Jesus was led by the Spirit into temptation whereas we pray that we might be delivered from temptation.

9. **Why do you think that is? What is special about Jesus?**

   Jesus is the only one who can fully resist all temptation. He is divine and can do nothing wrong. Hebrews 4:15-16 tells us that he has "been tempted in every way, just as we are—yet he did not sin", and that is why we can approach God with confidence to ask for help in times of need. Unlike Jesus, we need God's help to resist temptation. Because of Jesus, we have that help.

10. **Jesus' testing echoes the story of the fall in Genesis 3 and the story of the Israelites' time in the wilderness in Exodus (for example, Exodus 17:1-7).**

- **What are the similarities?**

  First, Jesus is tempted by Satan just as Adam was tempted by Satan in the Garden of Eden. Second, Jesus spends 40 days in the wilderness where he is tested, just as Israel spent 40 years in the wilderness where they are tested (Deuteronomy 8:2). Moreover, all Jesus' quotes come from Deuteronomy—the book written during those 40 years. In Exodus 17:2 and 7 the complaints of the people in the wilderness are said to test the Lord—the very thing Jesus refuses to do in Matthew 4:7.

- **What is the big difference?**

  Jesus passes the test whereas Adam and Israel failed. Jesus replays the story of humanity and the story of Israel. Uniquely, he passes Satan's test—and he does so on behalf of all his people. Through the faithfulness of Jesus, every Christian has passed the "entrance exam" required to enter God's kingdom.

11. **How do these passages illuminate what it means to pray to be delivered from evil?**

    Being delivered from evil means being delivered...

    - from doubts about the ability of Jesus to forgive our sins (9:4).
    - from storing up evil in our hearts (12:35).

- from the influence of an unbelieving culture (12:39).
- from failing to retain God's word in our hearts (13:19).
- from being among the people under Satan's influence who are heading for judgment (13:38).
- from murderous, adulterous and envious thoughts (15:19).
- from an unforgiving attitude (18:32).

12. **When we do fail and fall, how should we feel and respond?**

Christians may fail when tested and fall when tempted. This is why we must pray, "Lead us not into temptation, but deliver us from the evil one". We should hate to fail, so we should pray for help in resisting temptation. But failure is never final for Christians because Jesus has passed the test on our behalf. We can approach God's throne in confidence (Hebrews 4:16).

Explore the Whole Range

Old Testament, including:

 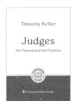  

Tim Chester — Exodus — *Liberating Love*

Timothy Keller — Judges — *The Flawed and the Flawless*

Kathleen B. Nielson and Rachel Jones — Proverbs — *Real Wisdom for Real Life*

David Helm — Daniel — *Staying Strong in a Hostile World*

New Testament, including:

 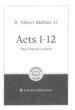  

Josh Moody — John 1-12 — *Life to the Full*

R. Albert Mohler Jr — Acts 1-12 — *The Church is Born*

Timothy Keller — Galatians — *Gospel Matters*

Michael Kruger — Hebrews — *An Anchor for the Soul*

Topical, including:

Carl Laferton — Promises Kept — *The Whole Story of the Bible*

Anne Woodcock — Joy — *Happiness of the Heart*

Jason Helopoulos — The Five Solas — *These Truths Alone*

Tim Chester — The Lord's Prayer — *Talking to Our Father*

Flexible and easy to use, with over 50 titles available,
Good Book Guides are perfect for both groups and individuals.

thegoodbook.com/gbgs
thegoodbook.co.uk/gbgs
thegoodbook.com.au/gbgs

GOOD BOOK GUIDE

BIBLICAL | RELEVANT | ACCESSIBLE

At The Good Book Company we are dedicated to helping Christians and local churches grow. We believe that God's growth process always starts with hearing clearly what he has said to us through his timeless and flawless word—the Bible.

Ever since we opened our doors in 1991, we have been striving to produce resources that are biblical, relevant, and accessible. By God's grace, we have grown to become an international publisher, encouraging ordinary Christians of every age and stage and every background and denomination to live for Christ day by day and equipping churches to grow in their knowledge of God, their love for one another, and the effectiveness of their outreach.

Call one of our friendly team for a discussion of your needs or visit one of our local websites for more information on the resources and services we provide.

Your friends at The Good Book Company